VOLKSWAGEN
CUSTOMS & CLASSICS

David A. Fetherston

MBI Publishing Company

For my brother Eric King
who ignited my boundless enthusiasm for life and Volkswagens . . .
Nanette – Fetherston Publishing.

First published in 1995 by MBI Publishing Company, PO Box 1, 729 Prospect Avenue, Osceola, WI 54020-0001 USA

© David A. Fetherston, 1995

MBI Publishing Company books are also available at discounts in bulk quantity for industrial or sales-promotional use. For details write to Special Sales Manager at Motorbooks International Wholesalers & Distributors, 729 Prospect Avenue, PO Box 1, Osceola, WI 54020-0001 USA.

Library of Congress Cataloging-in-Publication Data
Fetherston, David A.
    Volkswagen customs & classics/David A. Fetherston.
        p. cm. — (Enthusiast color series)
    Includes index.
    ISBN 0-87938-984-2
    1. Volkswagen automobile—History.   I. Title. II. Title: Volkswagen customs and classics. III. Series.
    TL215.V6F44   1995
    629.222—dc2094-44218

On the front cover: A fantastic 1958 Cal-bug created and owned by Troy Elwood.

On the frontispiece: A 1957 Window Bus restored and owned by Todd Hicks.

On the title page: This wildly flamed Beetle, owned by Will Stevens, is a composite of parts from '57 through '64 Beetles, plus '72.

On the back cover: Steve Wood's collection of classic Volkswagens: (clockwise from front left) a 1944 German Army Kübelwagen, 1951 Type 211 van, a 1951 Microbus, another 1951 Type 211 van, the real "Herbie," from the *Love Bug* movies, and a 1951 Type 1 Sedan.

Printed in Hong Kong

Contents

Acknowledgments   6

Introduction   7

Chapter 1   Stock Volkswagens   9

Chapter 2   Volkswagen Commercials   33

Chapter 3   Military Volkswagens   43

Chapter 4   Coachbuilt Volkswagens   47

Chapter 5   The Cal Look   53

Chapter 6   Baja and Buggies   75

Chapter 7   Kits   79

Chapter 8   Race Cars   91

Index   96

Acknowledgments

The VWs in this book have been collected over the past six-years for many magazine stories and specifically for this book. I would like to thank the many folks who gave me their time so that I could photograph all these great air-cooled VWs. I'd especially like to thank Keith Seume from Volks World in England and Jacky Morel from *Super VW* magazine in France for their help, along with the public relations folks at Volkswagen of America for their time and interest in helping us get historic photos for this book. I would also like to thank Jane Mausser for her assistance and persistence, Cori Ewing for his help with getting the text started, and Dr. Steve Werlin for handling the heart department. At Fetherston Publishing I could not have done this book without the help of Nanette Simmons and Gloria Fetherston, whose organization and editorial insights have brought this project to its completion.

Virtually all the photography I shot for the book was done on a Mamiya RB 6X7 Pro S camera system. It's a great machine. Once again all the film was Fuji RDP 100, superbly processed by The Lab in Santa Rosa, California.

Introduction

The Volkswagen Beetles are loved, hated, and referred to as Beetles and Bugs, Wobblies, Air-coolies, Slugs, Cal Look-ers, V-dubs, Krauts, Corn-poppers, Slug-bugs, and more.

But the little "Bug that could" has, by its very design as a "people's car," transported folks millions of miles year after year.

Its endearing happy shape is all part of the effect which, along with the simplicity of operation and mechanical assembly, turned many non-tool users into happy little grease monkeys.

I've owned my share of air-cooled VWs: five sedans of various years, three transporters, a 2.0 liter street racer with Porsche Turbo fenders, and a self-built Baja Bug. I purchased Series I and Series II Type 2 vans. The first was a 36-horse panel which I used as a photo equipment transporter; the second was a well used ex-commercial service van which came with all its company lettering still painted on its flanks.

Both did sterling service and took me on many interesting photographic and surfing adventures. My buddies also bought them. Rory, Robbo, Wazza, Shane, Mac, and Steve would pile into a couple of transporters to travel to distant surf spots. Our VW vans not only got us there, they provided cheap overnight accommodations and even cooking space. They were considered our friends and when one of them broke down everyone helped to get her back on the road. Our ex-commercial vans also enabled us to park any place we chose, they still looked official and no-one ever ticketed us for parking where we wanted.

My street racer was built from a 1972 sedan, motorless but with a perfect body, wide wheels, and new tires, for $250. My custom Bug was a Baja kit which I built out of an engine-less $25 roller. Other VWs came to my driveway for as low as $40 and went away selling for a lot more. They taught me about good engineering, simplicity of design, and gave me self confidence to pursue greater mechanical journeys with more expensive automobiles.

Bugs, I love 'em, and though it's a pity that they're no longer sold, there are plenty of old ones still around providing all of us with plenty of fun.

David Fetherston
Sonoma County, California

Chapter1

Stock Volkswagens

A Phoenix That Emerged From the Fire of War

The evolution of the Volkswagen is a convoluted tale of political intrigue, engineering genius, and a conviction that the car would be a success. It could have been "killed off" by a small handful of people at several critical points in its history, and the fact that the car survived after 1945 is a wonder unto itself.

The Volkswagen started out from the concepts put forward by several brilliant engineers including Edmund Rumpler, an aerodynamicist, Hans Ledwinka of the Tatra automobile company, and Ferdinand Porsche.

Ferdinand Porsche had started a design firm after leaving Steyr-Daimler-Puch in 1930. Many projects were forming and brilliant new designs were at hand but Steyr-Daimler-Puch was not the place for Porsche to pursue his ideas. Once free of the company he designed a fully independent torsion bar suspension and was granted a patent for it in August 1931, little knowing it would prove to be one of the most innovative suspensions of the twentieth century.

His first automobile design commission, a large two-door sedan with a cut-away sloping rear bodywork, was for the Wanderer Automobile Company. Ferdinand did the engineering and Edwin Komenda drew up the body design at Porsche's new Stuttgart studio. The project fell on hard times but Porsche was determined not to let the hard work go to waste. The rounded aerodynamic lines of the design were carried into a light car project the firm produced for the German motorcycle manufacturer Zündapp the following year.

The project went one step further with a new rear-engined prototype in 1932. The body wrapped down sharply at the rear, covering a water-cooled, five-cylinder 1.2 liter radial engine which was mounted behind the axle. It was designed around a backbone chassis with

The Beetle convertible has led an amazingly long life. The first production models emerged in 1946 and the last U.S. versions were sold in 1979. This superb 1963 Off White convertible has just been completed after three years of restoration. Originally delivered in Chicago, the current owner and restorer, Cal Jackson, did a "pan off," re-painting the convertible himself and bringing the interior up to show quality in stock off-white with a new Tan Hartz fabric convertible top.

When the 1935/36 Type 60 prototype arrived, it carried all the traits that would endure throughout the Beetle's life: platform pan chassis, torsion bar suspension, air-cooled rear engine, floating fenders, and basic body shape. Next to come were the Mercedes-built Series-30s which were certified after a million miles of twenty-four hours-a-day testing.

independent suspension using a transverse leaf up front and torsion bar swing axles in the rear. These design elements eventually flowed into the final VW design.

At the same time there were other forces playing heavily into this event which Porsche never envisaged. With a flurry of party banners and a slurry of dogmatic words, Hitler came to power in 1933.

Part of Hitler's political platform was to create a dream for the future of Germany. The country was an economic wreck, hurt by the demands for reparations from World War I and global depression. Germany needed jobs and industry and Hitler had a plan to provide both.

Part of that plan followed Henry Ford's creation of the Model T and Hitler's assump-

This 1949 show model may not have been the first Volkswagen Beetle to arrive in America, but the Dutch distributor, Ben Pon, brought it in to show off the line to the public and potential dealers. Max Hoffmann, the U.S. importer, became the agent in 1950 and sold 300 cars. A returning GI probably brought the first Volkswagen into the United States after the war.

tion that roads would be needed to carry the cars. His first most enduring and least tragic plan was the building of a set of "Autobahnen" – motorways. This project was to have a multi-fold effect – create tremendous employment across the country and lift the economy to a level where people could afford to buy "the people's car."

At his first cabinet meeting, Hitler introduced his plan for the Autobahnen and "people's car." Long on vision but short on engineering realities, Hitler laid out a list of requirements. The roads were to follow the same engineering ideas that the Italians had used with their "autostrade" motorways. Eventually this network of roads stretched over 2500 miles.

The history of this 1951 Type 1 Sedan runs through three countries. Built in Germany at Wolfsburg, it was sold in Brussels, Belgium the same year. It was found in storage in 1988, and restored by a Belgian VW collector. It was then sold to Bill Dierickx and imported to Seattle, Washington. Bill later sold it to Steve Wood, who collects only 1951 vintage Volkswagens.

The basic idea of the people's car followed a list of specifications which Hitler had prepared. The car had to be capable of reaching 62 mph (100 km/h) while getting the equivalent of 42 mpg, carry two adults and three children and cost less than 1000 Reichmarks ($150). He wanted it powered by an air-cooled engine.

Despite possessing only rudimentary knowledge of automobile design theory, Hitler sketched a drawing of the rounded front end that he desired for the car after he had seen some early design ideas.

Apparently Ferdinand Porsche did not willingly accept this government request but ultimately agreed to the project. The concept was in fact "a ghost" of his Zündapp Type 12 and the defunct NSU Type 32 prototypes. Therefore developing this new project was, for Porsche, rather simple. His only problem was the lack of a reliable air-cooled engine.

Several air-cooled engines were built and discarded but in 1934, Franz Xavier Reimspiess joined Porsche's design team. Reimspiess, a mechanical engineer, produced a design for a horizontally-opposed four-cylinder that drew as much from the motorcycle engine design as it did from automobile engineering. It was quickly apparent that this four-cylinder engine was far superior to the two-cylinder prototypes on which Porsche had been working.

By 1936, a handful of prototypes had been built and a trio of cars were tested by the German Automobile Manufacturers Association. However the cast iron crankshafts failed early in testing. The problem was solved within a short time when they converted to a conventional forged crank ordered from Daimler-Benz.

With this and other design problems solved, the German government took over the car in 1937 as a state-funded, German Labor Front project. Thirty prototypes were then built by Daimler-Benz for further testing. These Type 60 units had no back window and a large louvered panel covered the engine.

Edwin Komenda was then handed the project to complete the design. His job was to refine and simplify the styling. During the winter of 1937, the Reutter coach building company assembled a new version with a split back

oval window and a smaller trunk lid. Daimler-Benz was asked to build another series of fourty- four prototypes for testing and display.

Hitler apparently liked what he saw, and ordered the construction of a new factory in 1938 on the banks of the Mitterland Canal about fifty miles east of Hannover, Germany. Much to the disgust of Porsche, Hitler named the car "Kraft durch Freude: KdF-Wagen" which is German for "Strength through Joy." The factory town, called "Town of Strength through Joy Cars," was renamed "Wolfsburg" by the British.

The rear fender on Steve Wood's 1951 sedan is emblazoned with a large B for Belgium. This was required by law in Europe so police could quickly and easily identify the vehicle's country of origin.

Aux jours de vacances comme aux jours de travail...

une compagne fidèle...

Joignant l'agrément de la décapotable
à la solidité et l'étanchéité de la conduite
intérieure, la Volkswagen à toit ouvrant
affirme encore une fois le souci de perfec-
tionnements des usines Volkswagen!

Ⓥ VOLKSWAGEN

ANCIENS ETABLISSEMENTS D'IETEREN FRERES S.A.
BRUXELLES · 50, R. DU MAIL ·   LIEGE · 20, R. DES GUILLEMINS ·   CHARLEROI · 6, R. DE LA FENDERIE
TEL. 44.48.00   TEL. 43.01.12   TEL. 200.30 & 39
AGENCES DANS TOUT LE PAYS

This advertisement used by the Belgian VW distributor touted the Volkswagen Beetle as "A Faithful Companion" for travel to work, home, and leisure. Holland and Belgium were the first two export destinations for the VW Beetle. This is one of the earliest post-war ads we could find.

In order to finance the building of the factory, the Labor Front party began a program whereby individuals could purchase a KdF-Wagen by making deposits in a savings book. When the full purchase price had been deposited the buyer could take delivery. Needless to say, the program did not have the buyers' best interests in mind.

Not a single pre-war Volkswagen was delivered to a citizen as Hitler invaded Poland at the end of 1939, before the plant got into production. France and Britain, in honoring their treaties, declared war on Germany.

During the war only 640 Beetles were built. Production switched instead to the Kübelwagen, a war type body placed on the original VW platform. The Kübelwagen was the German equivalent to the American Jeep and proved almost as versatile, although it was produced in much smaller quantities.

The Kübelwagen was able to stand up to the extreme heat of Africa and the equally harsh cold of the Soviet Union without modifications. Rommel, the head of the Afrika Korps, did have some special

The second batch of export cars had this split window in 1952. They featured chrome hubcaps, quarter panel air vents, semaphore turn signals, and a single outlet exhaust.

This delightfully restored 1954 sedan features its original semaphore turn signals, U.S. specification headlights lenses, and twin outside mirrors. It's amazing how simple touches can come together so nicely when completing a restoration. The white wall tires and two-tone rims add a delightful touch to the car's crisp fresh character.

desert vehicles produced but they were inadvertently shipped to the Russian Front.

The Kübelwagen gained reduction hubs that halved the minimum speed to 2.5 mph hour, about the speed of a marching man, as

This sedan was imported and sold in January, 1955, yet it carries many 1954 features. Owned by Robert and Debbie McLear, it is still powered by a 36-horsepower 1200cc four. Finished in factory Black, this European sedan version came with semaphore turn signals, Hella fog lights, pop-out side windows, window shades, and an optional VW dealer roof rack.

well as raising the ground clearance. A number of specialized body types were produced from the Kübelwagen including an amphibious vehicle and various four-wheel drive versions.

Wartime production at the KdF-Wagen factory was not limited to vehicles. BMW airplane engine parts, spares, heat stoves for the frigid Russian front, and V1 rockets were all

Charles Sellers is a Volkswagen user and collector. He owns an extensive selection of early transporters and this 1956 Type 1, which he drives every day. Charles spent two years restoring this oval-windowed sedan into a driver, replacing the suspension software and refreshing the 36 horse motor. He selected red and beige and added dealer wheel trims and new overrider bumpers.

This Arctic Blue 1960 sedan is now with its third owner, Stan Smith, after the first and second owners put 93,000 miles on the clock. It was purchased from Henry Veale VW in Santa Rosa, California, in 1960 and serviced by them every 1,500 miles. It was so well cared for that the first set of bias-ply tires lasted 50,000 miles.

The only water a Volkswagen needs is the water you wash it with.

All car engines must be cooled. But how? Conventional cars are cooled by water. The Volkswagen engine is cooled by air.

The advantages are astonishing, when you think about it. Your Volkswagen cannot boil over in summer or freeze in winter, since air neither boils nor freezes.

You need no anti-freeze. You have no radiator problems. In fact, you have no radiator.

In midsummer traffic jams, your VW can idle indefinitely, while other cars and tempers boil.

The doughty Volkswagen engine is unique in still other ways. Its location in the rear means better traction (in mud, sand, ice, snow, where other cars skid, you go). And since it is cast of aluminum-magnesium alloys, you save weight and increase efficiency. Your VW delivers an honest 32 miles to the gallon, regular driving, regular gas.

And you will probably never need oil between changes.

built in large quantities, earning the factory a high priority for allied bombing runs.

With Germany's unconditional surrender in 1945, the war ended but KdF-Wagen production continued to trickle from the mostly destroyed factory. Several hundred Kübelwagens were assembled from spare parts and bodies still being shipped in from the Ambi-Budd body company in Berlin. English, French and American companies came to look at the strange little car as a possible war reparation item but all passed on it, feeling it to be a primitive little contraption with no future.

With the cessation of hostilities, KdF-Wagen officially became Volkswagen "The People's Car." The British administration took over the running of this sector of Germany.

Major Ivan Hirst of the Royal Electrical and Mechanical Engineers was appointed to KdF-Wagen to see if it was worth saving for reparations or, if not, to see if he could re-start the company.

Rarely has a Phoenix risen from the ashes and ruins in a more spectacular fashion than did Volkswagen following the devastation of World War II. To go from a crushed company with over seventy-five percent of its factory destroyed, and ownership in doubt, to the largest European manufacturer and producer of the most popular car ever, is truly one of the most impressive feats of the twentieth century.

It was Ivan Hirst's drive for getting the show back on the road that was the spark that set the place rolling again. Beyond the internal difficulties of rebuilding the factory and determining leadership and ownership, raw materials were scarce, although labor was plentiful.

Hirst scrounged and scraped together enough materials and parts to get a few cars into production and started a rebuilding program at the factory. By March 1946 the 1000th Volkswagen was being driven off the production line.

By mid-1948 the Volkswagen factory was once again in full swing, and rolled out their 30,000th vehicle. Hirst helped to appoint Heinz Nordhoff as general manager and in 1949 the ownership of the company was transferred to the German government and then to the State of Lower Saxony.

One of Major Hirst's aspirations for VW included commercial vehicles and during his time with the company he had the shop produce prototype Beetle pickups and sedan deliveries which were used around the plant.

In 1948 at the instigation of Ben Pon, the Dutch VW distributor, Nordhoff initiated a project to develop a commercial delivery van based on Beetle mechanicals, and in 1950 the Transporter Type 2 Van was in production.

By 1950 Volkswagen was Germany's largest manufacturer, producing almost fifty percent of the country's automobiles. Nordhoff improved quality and expanded his product line offerings.

Right top: When Shawn DeLuna saw this sedan its only appealing points were its vintage and the fact that it ran. The body was pockmarked all over from twenty-six years of everyday abuse and the interior looked like dogs had been using it for shelter. After driving it for a short time he started on a major restoration. The suspension, brakes, and steering were brought back to delivery day condition with a combination of restored original parts, NOS, and stock new factory items. The body was stripped to a basic shell and then hammered to perfection so Alioto's Body Shop in San Francisco could add a lustrous coat of VW Olympic Blue and Almond. New glass and door rubbers were installed and the interior was redone in white leatherette and original Ora Wheat carpet as specified for a 1961 US export sedan. The 1192cc four still delivers a hearty 40 horsepower with its vacuum advance distributor, 6 volt electrical system, and 28mm Solex downdraft carburetor. Shawn spent many hours locating the correct original style accessories including a flag pole with flag for the right front fender, a set of headlight eyebrows and beam splitters, a tail pipe connector, radio, a wicker parcel shelf, and a wood slatted roof rack. The end result is "ten of ten" for a VW restoration that has proven to be both fun to drive and a joy to the eyes.

Stan Smith's 1960 looks just like it did the day it left the showroom. Virtually everything about this car, including the paint, is original. The interior is perfect and totally original including an optional fuel gauge. Stan disassembled and cleaned every surface of this sedan to give it its "like new" appearance.

Right bottom: By the beginning of the sixties, the Volkswagen Beetle had grabbed large chunks of the small car market all over the world. They were not only being built in Germany but in Australia, South Africa, and South America. In 1962 the Beetle arrived with larger taillights and a new PVC emissions system on the engine. It also came with seat

belt mounting points, pressurized windshield washers, and a new steering box using a worm and roller arrangement. When Jeff Whitten from Gilroy, California, found this 1962 sedan it was a junker but within eighteen months he had restored it to superb condition in Gulf Blue and White and now has it rolling on white walled tires.

Volkswagen, Italian style.

The Karmann Ghia goes to show you what happens when you turn a Volkswagen over to an Italian designer.

It comes out with a noble Roman nose, graceful curves, and a low silhouette.

In fact, classical tradition is followed right down the line.

Fenders, hoods and door frames are welded and shaped and smoothed by hand.

Seats and convertible tops are padded and stitched and fitted by hand.

Now you might think we're crazy to go to all this trouble, just to turn out some fancy Italian sculpturing.

Especially since this body of work ends up on top of one of those plain VW chassis. But consider.

The chassis includes VW's 4-speed syn-chromesh transmission, big 15-inch wheels, torsion bars, and an easy-to-service non-temperamental engine.

So that with the Ghia's beautiful form and this strictly functional interior, you've got yourself a pretty solid piece of architecture.

It's known as renaissance Volkswagen.

William Bernbach was the creator of these ads from the Doyle Dane Bernbach advertising agency and even his Karmann-Ghia ads were humorous, suggesting that it was "a German-Italian beauty with a noble Roman Nose."

Donna Peterson's 1966 convertible appears to be a clean and stock "droptop." Interestingly, long before her ownership a former owner had crashed the car and replaced the front sheet metal with 1962 fenders and a 1960 hood. These, combined with the Light Green paintwork, give this Karmann-bodied convertible the appearance of an earlier model. Eric Birky performed an extensive restoration on the car and decided to leave the body as it was because it gave the car a stock, yet classic, look.

He contracted with Karmann in Osnabrück to build a production Cabriolet and with Hebmüller of Wülfrath to build a factory-approved two-seater convertible. Surprisingly, the Karmann Cabriolet outlasted the sedan production but the two-seater Hebmüller disappeared within four years after a disastrous factory fire.

In 1950, when the 100,000th vehicle had been built, Nordhoff looked to the export market for further sales. Beetles were being sold in Germany, Austria, Belgium, and Holland but Nordhoff could see vast sales possibilities in America.

The history of "The Thing" is one of failure and triumph. It was designed as a modern "Kübelwagen" or Light Field Car for the German Army and NATO but in field testing it proved to be out of its depth against its four-wheel-drive competitors. However, VW was not so quick to kill it off. They moved the project to their Mexico assembly plant and started a production run in 1969 that ran until 1974. Powered by a dual-port 46 horsepower 1600cc, it used Transporter rear suspension and transmission. These Mexican assembled Things were sold in the United States and there is now a resurgence of interest due to their increasing rarity. This factory original Orange 1974 model belongs to Mark Merrill from Atherton, California. It is nicely restored and fitted with optional Acapulco-style running boards and sliding glass windows in the front doors.

What is it?

Glad you asked.
It's a Volkswagen Station Wagon.
Don't pity the poor thing; it can take it.
It can carry nearly a ton of anything you can afford to buy.
Or 8 people (plus luggage) if you want to get practical about it.
And there's more than one practical consideration.
It will take you about 24 miles on a gallon of regular gas.
It won't take any water or anti-freeze at all; the engine is air-cooled.
And even though it carries almost twice as much as regular wagons, it takes 4 feet less to park.
What's in the package?
8 pairs of skis, the complete works of Dickens, 98 lbs. of frozen spinach, a hutch used by Grover Cleveland, 80 Hollywood High gym sweaters, a suit of armor, and a full sized reproduction of the Winged Victory of Samothrace.

Bernbach's Volkswagen Station Wagon ad asked "What is it?" leaving the viewer to decide whether he was asking about the van or the object wrapped up inside.

He encouraged Ben Pon to take a Volkswagen to America. Ben's trip was unproductive and he sold only one car. The following year, in New York, Max Hoffmann was appointed as the U.S. importer, but after selling only 601 cars in two years this arrangement was cancelled. Volkswagen tried again in 1955 and opened "Volkswagen of America" offices. Finally America was ready to own VWs and more than 30,000 vehicles were sold. By this time Volkswagen had built their one millionth car.

By 1953 the classic "split" window was replaced by an oval window and in 1955 semaphore turn signals were lost to the past when flashing turn signals were added. Many small improvements were made to the basic design: interior trims were revised, engine details were improved, lights were

Left: In 1976 America was celebrating its Bicentennial Year. Many companies produced special products to highlight the year. Volkswagen of America was one of them and this 1976 Bicentennial Convertible belonging to John Ryan was the third car made of a 1000 model run. It features factory fender skirts, foglights, Fan Fare horns, console, gauge package, deluxe radio, and extra lights for the trunk and engine compartment. It also features chrome factory wheels and a host of other smaller accessories. John purchased the car from its original owner and now drives and shows the convertible at Bug shows in Northern California. We found him at the Lakeport Bug Fest.

Volkswagen chose 1985 to celebrate its 50th Anniversary with this Special. It was packaged with pressed steel wheels, impact bumper, a special color, interior trim, and quarter panel trim tags.

modified, switches and bumpers were changed, options were added, and instruments were redesigned. The Type 2 transporter range was also expanded to include pickup and crew-cab models.

Other models were also commissioned. Volkswagen had Ghia in Italy design a sporty

The Type 3 lasted thirteen years on the American Market before it was replaced by the water-cooled Rabbit. Introduced in 1961, the Type 3 was originally intended to be sold as a replacement for the Beetle but sales for the Beetle were so strong that the company decided to build the Type 3 as a separate model line. The Type 3 was introduced to the American market for the 1965-66 model year and were sold until 1973 in only Squareback wagon and Fastback configurations. A sedan version was sold in other markets but a few sedans have been privately imported into the States over the years. This 1971 Clementine Orange Squareback wagon, owned by Larry Torrey from Lakeport, California, is used as his daily driver and is powered by its original fuel injected 1600 engine.

coupe and cabriolet based on the export chassis and contracted with Karmann to build them. The coupe arrived in 1955 and the cabriolet came two years later. The Karmann-Ghia's classic lines echoed the Beetles' shapes and made it a popular variation which sold all over the world. It arrived in the U.S. in 1956 and 2,500 were sold.

The oval window Beetle lasted to the end of 1957 when the new large rear window 1958 model was introduced. By this stage the Beetle was selling up a storm in the United States. Sales had reached 50,000 units and Volkswagen had a nation-wide dealer network which was backed up with a good service and parts supply. The company was also deep into an ongoing advertising campaign which snapped not only the public's attention, but also the attention of the advertising industry with its simplistic but hard hitting approach.

Sales continued to crest each previous year's totals and in 1961 Volkswagen introduced the Type 3. Nordhoff felt that the Beetle had a finite life and the company needed to develop a replacement. The Type 3 was the result but with sales of the Beetle continuing to rise, Nordhoff held off introducing the car for four years. The Type 3 continued production alongside the Type 1 until 1973 and was sold all over the world as a sedan, a wagon, and a fastback.

The least successful air-cooled model, the Type 4, was introduced in 1968 and lasted only six years. It was Volkswagen's first four-door model and sold poorly because of its strange design.

The Type 181, "The Thing," was introduced in 1969 for use by the German Armed Forces. The Thing wanted to be the successor to the wartime Kübelwagen but lacked technical refinement and strength to make it useful. The four-wheel drive was missing and only the first few examples had the reduction hubs of the earlier vehicles.

The military rejected The Thing but VW could see other sales opportunities. They moved production to Mexico and began selling it there, exporting them to the United States and South American countries. Exports continued from 1972 through 1979.

By the end of 1982 no air-cooled VWs were being sold in the United States; the last model to carry an air-cooled flat-four was the Third Series, Type 2 Vanagon.

The new generation of Volkswagens have all been "waterpumpers" which have evolved into vastly more complex vehicles that offer combinations of power and luxury not even contemplated when the "people's car" was envisaged. These new Volkswagens have sold in vast numbers across the globe but have yet to surpass the mark of ninety million air-cooled Beetles sold.

While no air-cooled Volkswagens remain in either the European or American new car market, they are still being driven off Brazilian and Mexican production lines. How long this production will continue no one knows as the Beetle makes perfect sense for emerging nations' economies.

Though the fate of the world's best selling car continues to sail along like a feather on the winds of time, its spirit will live in the new Volkswagen Concept I prototype which has received tremendous accolades from the press. The people's car was a dream fulfilled and judging by the ongoing interest in the marque, Beetles and all their derivations will continue to be "Joy Cars" for their owners.

Chapter 2

Volkswagen Commercials

Volkswagen's concept to sell a basic line of models was its saving grace during the early years. The decision to expand the product line was taken seriously by Heinz Nordhoff, the company's general manger. Ben Pon, the Dutch VW importer, had shown Nordhoff his concept of building a commercial transporter van based on Type 1 mechanicals. Nordhoff apparently had similar inklings and proceeded to develop the concept which was finally introduced in 1950 as the Type 2 Transporter van.

Ken Munc's perfect Cal Look bus is hard to beat for style and usefulness. Ken acquired this 1967 Kombi Van from its original owner who had purchased it at the Volkswagen factory in Hanover, Germany, complete with sunroof option. Hanover was the site of the Transporter line since its introduction in 1956. When Ken got it a few years ago he started on a complete "Cal-resto" conversion with Safari windows and a roof rack. The suspension is lowered via a modified suspension from Bus Boys of Redding, California, and the Kombi now rolls on Empi 5-spoke alloy wheels capped with 195-60/15 tires. The interior is fully customed with white and turquoise trimming complimenting the exterior colors. It is powered by a fully detailed, modified 1600cc.

It was an immediate hit with small businesses. Variations soon evolved including a pickup, a double-cab, a camper, the Kombi, and the Microbus. By the end of the first model production run in 1967 two million had been sold. In 1968 the Series II Type 2 Transporter was introduced with a full-line up of models from high top to double-cab, to camper and Kombi.

Eleven years later, in 1979, the Third Series Type 2 replaced it with a similar line-up. This generation of Transporter carried the final fuel-injected air-cooled Volkswagen engines sold in the United States. In 1983 they were replaced by the "Wasserboxer" water-cooled flat-four in the same body.

Today Volkswagen commercials are extremely popular with the Cal Look set. "Slammed vans" top the list when painted in stock pastel colors and fitted with Porsche five-spoke alloy wheels. Bumper stickers on these transporters read "Low is Slow" and "Slammed," appropriate titles for these ground-scraping wagons which can behead an ant.

The semaphore turn signals on Steve Wood's Prandtner textile company Type 2 van flip in and out to indicate turning direction. Semaphore turn signals were common on European and British vehicles before World War II. They were used for about ten years after the war, then flashing turn signals replaced them.

Steve Wood has been a vintage VW collector for many years. His collection of pre-1955 Volkswagens is seen elsewhere in this book. This 1951 Type 211 was a classic restoration which features the factory lettering from the Prandtner textile company in Germany who were the original purchasers of this van. It is painted in two-tone and like all these early vans it features a one-piece rear door which opens up the back of the van and the engine compartment together. It also features semaphores, a single bumper, Safari windows, factory mirrors, and matching two-tone wheels and hub caps.

Above: Steve Wood's German Fire Truck Transporter was built on a 1951 Microbus by an outside supplier of fire apparatus for the small German town of Alberdsdorf. It uses a 1131cc, 25 horsepower VW industrial engine to power a water pump mounted in the back of the van. The pump is mounted on a stretcher-like carrier so that two men can remove the portable pump and motor and carry it close to the fire. Hoses were then connected to the pump and the fire could be extinguished.

Right: This 1960 Transporter truck was sold new to a vineyard in Mendecino County, California. It was used around the vineyard until the engine seized in 1968, and then it sat for the next twenty-five years beside a barn on the farm. Eric Birky purchased it early in 1993 and stripped it to a shell. He rebuilt the body by removing some rust and restoring the doors, fold-down bed panels, and the storage compartments. It is finished in its original Dove Blue and powered by the correct 1200cc commercial four.

Left: Todd Hicks wanted to build "The Baddest Bus in Town" so he tackled this 1957 Window Bus as a challenge. He stripped it to a shell, repaired the abused bodywork and removed the normal bus rust. He then sent it to Don Serrano at Serrano Design who laid out the graphics to balance with the natural curves around the nose of the van. He ran the graphics up and into the side molding and then into the rear side panel "Z." The front torsion bar assembly was modified with a ride height adjustable conversion and the transaxle was replaced with a 1967 sedan unit with straight axles. The gearbox was modified with a Beef-A-Diff spider gear set and the van now uses 1965 Type III brakes. Center Line alloy wheels add to the dropped effect making up a hefty ten inch drop for the Bus. Inside, the detail and stunning colors flow into a custom interior of hot pink and turquoise with a white sunroof and the carpet in hot pink with white piping. The motor displaces 1853cc and uses a pair of 44mm IDF Weber carburetors on Weber manifolds.

Above: The sixties was the time when Americans, Australians, and New Zealanders discovered that touring Europe was fun and cheap. One of the favorite modes of transportation was VW Kombi vans with the best option being a Westfalia camper version. The Westfalia came with beds, cupboards, table, cooler, and stove and was VW's first commercially successful RV. This 1966 Westfalia Bus was purchased new in Germany and driven all over Europe for a year. It was then imported to the United States by its first owners. Powered by its original 1500cc four, the camper is still fully equipped and is used by its owner, Eric Birky, for occasional camping trips.

39

Bill Bledsoe's 1967 Cal-Bus has collected enough trophies to start a trophy shop. His wins include the Grand National Roadster Show in Oakland, California, but that's not unusual as this Bus has all the tricks from Raspberry paint to wild pink graphics. Powered by a 1776cc four which has been decorated with chrome and colored detailing, the Bus rocks to the power of a super mega watt sound system. Bill drives his Raspberry Bus to many Northern California events, taking advantage of the Safari windows for cooling during hot summer days.

This super looking Double Cab Pickup was photographed at "Bugs By the Bay" in Vallejo, California, which is one of the excellent shows produced by the Goodguys show folks. The Type 2 was hammered smooth, painted in a delicious Cerise and White, and slammed and fitted out with polished Porsche five-spokes. It was fitted with chromed bumpers front and rear and an optional VW roof rack.

This shortened Bus was photographed at the Mooneyes Street Car Nationals in Japan. Its name is Short Delivery and it belonged to a Volkswagen restoration shop named Bug Fender. The owner loved driving it about with its perfect multi-colored paintwork, chromed Porsche 356 wheels, body colored hubcaps, and Safari windows.

Chapter 3

Military Volkswagens

The start of World War II was a signal for Germany to convert from civilian production to building military equipment. Only two military Volkswagens were built at the KdF factory: The Kübelwagen and the Schwimmwagen. This factory, in the "Town of the Strength through Joy Cars," was quickly tooled up to create the military application KdF Type 82 or Kübelwagen. This general purpose military personnel carrier used Porsche's engineering concepts to create an off-road, go anywhere, German type two-wheel drive Jeep. A four-wheel drive version was added later along with a limited number of sedans with two and four-wheel drive.

Apart from the new "open scout car" body there were several significant running changes to the production line equipment for the Kübelwagen. It featured a larger capacity 1130cc engine which produced 25hp, and the transaxle was revised with a smaller, lighter transmission with a limited-slip differential and reduction boxes fitted into the wheel hubs.

The Kübelwagen set in motion ideas that have rolled forward for fifty years without much change. The object of the Kübelwagen was to be a lightweight "go-anywhere" military utility vehicle that could be produced quickly, was reliable, and serviced easily. When Rommel set out across the deserts of North Africa to fight "die Englischen Schweinehunde," he had no idea that these vehicles would spawn a series of imitators continuing for decades. Steve Wood had dreams of owning a real "Kübe" for years and as luck would have it, he found this one not ten miles from his home in Seattle, Washington. His Kübelwagen turned out to be a 1944 T-82 version that was produced on May 2nd and delivered on May 4th, 1944, to the Heereszeugamt/Kassel (Army Auto Office) a month before the D-Day landings on the Normandy coast. Steve arranged for the vintage Volkswagen restoration expert Dave Crompton in Clio, Michigan, to do a top to bottom, nose to tail, restoration. The engine is a 25 horsepower unit built in 1943 with engine number 2-32238. The gearbox is a pre-synchro "crash-box" four speed. The restoration required new seats, floor boards, canvas top, and side curtains. Dave either replicated these from existing parts which came with the vehicle or copied the pieces from other Kübelwagens he had already restored.

According to several sources, about 48,000 of these two-wheel drives were manufactured and less than 800 four-wheel drive models were built before production stopped in mid-1945. The Kübelwagen has often been compared to the Jeep. In the European campaign it did well but in North Africa and Russia the Jeep was the star car.

The Type 166 Schwimmwagen was the most exotic deviation of air-cooled KdF/VW ever invented. This amphibious "swimming car" featured a boat-like body with seating for four, a fold down propeller, and four-wheel drive.

It was designed for the Russian Front where the severe weather and rugged terrain required fording of the many streams and rivers which confronted the Germans as they pushed their advance on Moscow. The swimming function of the Type 166 was achieved by lowering the collapsible propeller unit at the rear after the vehicle had entered the water. It was driven through a gearbox off the main crank pulley using a dog clutch for engagement.

The Schwimmwagen was not a great model in military terms but certainly served its purpose when the need called for crossing smooth and still waters found in lakes. Using it to cross flowing rivers and rough water was nearly impossible. More than 15,000 of these Type 166 Schwimmwagens were built during the war.

Some folks might add "The Thing" to the military Volkswagen list—it was designed for

military use, however it never served in any military application other than testing and was later transferred to Mexico for production. It is now considered a regular production model.

The Schwimmwagen was designed as the German military go-anywhere scout car with four-wheel-drive and amphibious capabilities. It had a rounded hull which also served as the lower bellypan, and floated like a small boat. A fold-down propeller was driven right off the end of the crank via a dog clutch. Apparently it was very slow in the water with a top speed of less than four knots and handled like a drunken sailor looking for a new bar. Also known as Type 166, the Schwimmwagen was built between 1942 and 1944 and despite intensive allied bombing more than 15,000 were built in the factory. This original 1942 model was found in a French monastery seven years ago and is owned by Bruce Crompton in England. *Norman Hodson photo*

Chapter 4

Coachbuilt Volkswagens

The impact of the aftermarket on VWs is a significant part of its history. Companies such as Hebmüller, Rometsch, Denzel, Dannenhauser, Strauss, Karmann, and others uplifted Volkswagens beyond their simple "people's car" image.

These coachbuilt Beetles provided a simple way of expanding the offerings in the showroom. Models such as the Hebmüller rebodied the car from the cowl back and production of this two-seater convertible ran out to about 700 units between 1949 and 1952. Several variations of the Hebmüller cars were built including a coupe and a drop-head convertible coupe. Rometsch followed Hebmüller using their new bodies on the VW pan. More luxurious and sporty looking than the Heb-

müller, the Rometsch was built in Berlin and sold throughout most of the fifties. It eventually evolved into four different models until the company quit production in 1961.

Another attempt came from Denzel, a performance parts manufacturer in Austria. He built approximately 150 cars at about the same time as Rometsch, using a custom aluminum sports car body powered by one of his modified flat-fours. Far more rare are models from small companies such as Strauss, Eller, Dannenhauser, and Drews.

The most successful of these coachbuilt cars was from the Karmann-Ghia team. The name signified the designer and the builder and during its twenty year production life over 300,000 coupes and convertibles were assembled. "The House of Ghia" was started in Turin, Italy, in 1915 by Giacinto Ghia and grew to be one of the auto industry's most respected design studios. Giacinto died during the Second World War and company leadership passed into the hands of a young designer, Mario Boano.

Boano re-created the company's image beginning in the early fifties. Ghia was work-

Hebmüller built just under 700 convertibles between 1949 and 1952. The production run ended when the factory was destroyed by fire in 1952. This nicely proportioned convertible is possibly the finest example of VW coachbuilding. Its beautifully clean lines came from a one-off design built at the Volkswagen factory in 1948. This recently restored, slick black and yellow example owned by Darryl Adams has taken many first place prizes in vintage VW shows on the East Coast. *Jackie Morel photo*

Right: Marc Harris is a vintage VW specialist and his great fascination with them began with the specialty coachbuilders who sold production cars built on VW platforms. His faded red and white 1957 Rometsch coupe is unrestored and driven daily. This extremely rare coupe had been in storage for many years when Marc found and purchased it recently. Marc researched it and discovered that it was the 14th built in 1957 of the second generation Rometsch coupes. Fredrich Rometsch halted production in 1962 when the Berlin wall went up as half his workers lived in the Eastern side of the city and could no longer get to work.

When you want to do a perfect job, you need time. Bill Yeager discovered this when he started on his 1959 convertible. Five years later this show winner has "knocked 'em in the aisles" with its wonderfully detailed interior, body, engine, and undercarriage. It is painted in Mango Green and rolls on 15in white-walled Firestones. Details on Bill's Ghia include Fan Fair horn, deck lid grille trims, 100,000 KM badge, fuel reserved extension, arm rest, reverse light, and dealer side badge. The convertible retains its stock 1100cc, 36 hp four but that doesn't slow it down one bit—this Karmann-Ghia lives in the fast lane.

This Type 143 Karmann-Ghia has an international story to tell. Built in Germany in March, 1959, it was delivered to a U.S. serviceman stationed in Japan. He brought it back to the U.S. and sold it to another serviceman. Richard Troy from Oakland, California, now owns this Ivory coupe which is fitted with a long list of factory accessories and engine performance items including an Empi suspension package, VDO instruments, and an Okrasa high performance engine kit with twin-carburetors. Inside the coupe is a locking shifter, a Blaupunkt multi-band radio, and Leatherite upholstery and carpeting.

Like many Karmann-Ghias, this one has been owned by only two or three people. Paul and Tracy Jones purchased this 1973 yellow convertible from the second owner who had just restored it. It features its original 65 horsepower 1600cc four which has been completely refreshed along with the body, paint, and interior. The convertible features U.S. specification impact bumpers, front disc brakes, and wrap-around turn signal lights. This was also the last production year for the traditional Karmann-Ghia coupe or convertible.

ing extensively with Chrysler on their new concept cars designed by Virgil Exner. It was Exner's influence, with his rounded flowing lines and fins, which helped to create an atmosphere in which the design of the Karmann-Ghia could evolve.

It is claimed that Boano down-sized one of Exner's concept cars to produce the Karmann-Ghia but I find this doubtful in that Boano was a classic automotive designer. Apparently there was some cooperation on the design and both Exner and Boano can claim a slice of the design cake. It was a tidy design with a high beltline and a cute rounded glasshouse. The pillars were thin and the window shapes flowed beautifully with the key elements of the body design.

When it was introduced in 1955 the Karmann-Ghia was quite a sensation. First to arrive in America were the 1956 models which sold for slightly under $2,400.

Like the Beetle, the Karmann-Ghia model changed very little until 1972. A convertible arrived with revised headlights in 1957 and there were minor changes in brakes, suspension, bumper trim, and engine size but basically the Karmann-Ghia, which started in 1955, stayed the same vehicle until it ceased production in 1974.

The Karmann-Ghia 1500, based on the Type 3 platform, was not as successful but did sell over 40,000 units during its eight year production run starting in 1962. It was a strange angular shape which still looked like a Ghia design, but had lost the basic cuteness of the original design.

The big bodied Type 34 1500 Karmann-Ghia never established itself in the market place like the earlier version. It was designed and prototyped by Sergio in 1959 but was not produced until 1962. A convertible version was also prototyped but never put into production. The coupe sold poorly; only a few were imported and total production for the model ran to just over 42,400 units by the time it was dropped in 1969.

Chapter 5

The Cal Look

If "cleanliness is next to godliness" then it must follow that the clean and pure Cal Look was destined to become an automotive religious movement. It arose in the seventies, flowed into the eighties, and continues on to this day.

Air-cooled Volkswagens have found homes in the garages and driveways of countless owners over the past fifty years and today their devotees follow a faithful path towards the smooth and clean life that all of us should lead.

The Volkswagen has turned out to be the perfect car for customizing. Not only are strong running examples abundant at a reasonable price but the cars respond well to style and performance modifications. What better home could a movement find than in California?

California has been the birthplace of many modern automotive trends from early racing activities, to customs, hot rods, mini-trucks, and VW. Even the hippie movement of the sixties chose the Volkswagen Kombi as their official mode of transportation.

Without realizing it, Volkswagen created a unique space. Not only did folks commute millions of miles in them every year but the car hobby, drag racing, and kit car industry also realised they would make a great base for a plethora of conversions.

Kit car companies like Devin and FiberFab created VW conversions which bolted straight onto a complete VW pan. In the mid-sixties Bruce Meyers created his wonderful Meyers

Julio and Frank Faraudo have been involved with air-cooled engines for years, first with VWs, then with aircraft engines and later with Porsches, so when Julio began building a tool-around-town Bug he decided it wasn't going to be just another plain Jane 1600. He took a stock '63 sedan and blended together an oval window, factory sliding sunroof, and a four inch chop. The fenders were replaced by 1967 models with special light units and then Frank applied a slick coat of Mustang Candy Apple Red. Inside, the VW parts sourcing continues with Scirocco seats converted to work on stock Bug rails. New door panels in velour and vinyl were also custom tailored. Julio installed a 1971 1600cc which has been opened out to 1854cc and fitted with a pair of Delorto's twin throat down-draft carburetors. Built to suit its owner's dreams, this Bug is a daily driver, mixing heaven and the highway into a wild-looking ride.

The first time I saw this wildly flamed Beetle it was doing about 80mph in the other direction. Five months later I came across it parked at a body shop called "Will, Power and Paint" in Santa Rosa, California. The owner was Will Stevens and his Beetle is one of the most innovative of its type ever built. It features custom tubular A-arms front suspension and a re-set rear suspension which keeps the ride quality right without destroying the handling. The roof has been chopped three inches with the stock rag top retained. Inside, the car has been completely customed with Recaro seats, leather wheel, custom dash, and carpet. It's powered by a heavily worked 2.0 liter four featuring dual down draft Webers, trick heads, and custom exhaust which exits ahead of the rear wheel. It is finished in black lacquer with the wildest set of flames I have ever seen on a VW – yellow, orange, and red with bright blue pinstriping. What year is this car? It has parts from 1957 through 1964 models, plus 1972!

Bill Orsborn's wild looking 1956 Cal Look Beetle is a perfect combination of color, craftsmanship, and style. Sitting on a 1967 pan, the Beetle has been shaved of door handles and trim and fitted with Porsche 911 light lenses. It rolls on polished 15x6in Porsche 911 alloy wheels while the suspension is set up with dropped spindles and re-set spring plates. The interior trimming matches the exterior with a super color blend of blue fabrics complimenting the stunning Candy Blue exterior. Power is supplied via a 1904cc flat-four which was built using all the hi-pop tricks. These include Cima pistons, Engle cam, racing heads, and twin Delorto carburetors. It's cool, crisp, and very slick. Need I say more?

Top: One of the neat features building Cal Look Bugs is their simplicity. Jeremy Smith, from San Jose, California, gave this 1957 Type 1 Beetle a superb Cal Look treatment with a few simple touches. It started out as a $700 project car and two years later features a dropped suspension, polished Porsche five-spoke alloy wheels, white fender piping, single blade bumpers, headlight visors, and white window rubber. The body is re-done in Mint Green with a white side panel and polished aluminum running boards, a factory rag top, and full blast sound system.

Bottom: Zane Cullen happens to be "a bit of a Leonardo" when it comes to body and paint work so when his wife, Stephanie, brought home a slightly mangled 1957 Bug, Zane shaped the roof, added a new front and rear aprons, spliced in a new vent section below the rear window, and repaired the rocker panels. He then started his own custom program. Off came the trim, emblems, door, and hood handles. Stephanie chose the color and Zane sprayed the car with Pastel Peach Deltron Urethane. A fully-dressed 1600cc engine, built and balanced by Bob Safinick of Petaluma, California, with ported and polished dual-port heads topped with dual 34mm Webers was then installed. The block is color coded in Peach to match the body as is the fan shroud and the alternator. Zane fitted an adjustable height front end and re-set the rear. The wheel package uses 15in polished American Eagle alloys capped with Kleber tires. Velour is used for the interior material and covers most of the surface area. Dark grey carpeting allows the lighter shade of grey fabric covering the '88 Honda Prelude bucket seats to add to the interior's accents. This "Peach Puppy" has taken home a goodly share of prizes at outdoor and indoor shows but soon it's going to be back to summer driving, just the way all good Cal-Bugs should be enjoyed.

Troy Elwood knows it's hard to play bug one-upmanship when your buddy, Eric Birky, builds a Cal-bug that hits the cover of every VW magazine on the newsstand. However, it gave him plenty of incentive and allowed him to cheat a little when it came to doing his own, by having Eric and Arnold Birky do the bodywork for him. Using a complete 1958 cabriolet, the body was hammered into a perfect shape with shaved trim and door handles, door and rear windows sills filled, rear fenders shaved, and the taillights changed to custom lights fitted into the rear bumper, along with European headlights up front. The roof was then chopped three inches and rebuilt so it would still fold like the conventional factory top. The chassis is modified with an Adjust-A-Drop at the front and a simple torsion bar re-set at the rear. A set of Japanese SL25 alloy wheels painted in matching body color add turbine styling to the Bug. Inside, the cool custom work continues. Troy started with a bare shell and added back his pieces one by one. The interior is also full custom with VDO instruments, billet door handles, and steering column.

Manx dune buggy which sold over 6,000 units during its two and one half years of production.

When it comes to automotive trends, vehicle owners try to outdo what a manufacturer has built for sale. The early years of custom cars in the fifties created a style from which the Cal Look VW has developed. The shaved and decked bodies of '50 Mercurys have long been a source of inspiration to car freaks and with the custom car trend flowering again, an increase in the number of new fifties style customs is occurring at shows.

The Cal Look is an extension of this idea and, when it first appeared, initial press opinion was very favorable. In February 1975, the Cal Look was officially named on the cover of *Dune Buggies and Hot VWs*. The magazine called the new style "The California Look" and featured a white Cal Look Bug belonging to Jim Holmes, devoid of side trim but revamped with Empi wheels, a rag top, nerf bars, and a quasi-legal suspension height.

This cover car had been built by Greg Aronson and featured a picture of Jim's Cal Look Bug being measured for legal street height by a member of Orange County's police force. Aronson and Ron Fleming built a motor with a 1700cc displacement through the use of 88mm barrels and pistons, an Engle 110 Camshaft, a Bosch 009 distributor, and dual 48IDA Weber carburetors. This assembly of parts became the standard for a Cal Look engine.

By this time the dune buggy industry had flowered and quietly faded into the background.

Power for Troy Elwood's custom 1958 Cabriolet is supplied via a custom built 1776cc flat four assembled by GEX in Baldwin Park, California. Troy trimmed the engine with chrome tinware, orange highlight paint color, and a chromed shroud.

However, from this point on the Cal Look idea grew into an international movement with many segments, one of the most interesting being the development in England and Europe.

In Hawaii they call the Cal Look "Island Style" and this is where the term "Local Motion" came from in connection with the Bug and Ghia custom look. The Hawaiians have their own style of car and have been trend setters for the mainlanders to follow. A day spent on the strip in Honolulu or at one of the VW events in

Dave Ruiz's chopped top 1960 cabriolet is done to a tee. From its Euro blade bumpers and custom taillights to its widened fenders, Gotti alloy wheels and 2.3 liter flat-four, this Bug is right on the money. Dave has won several trophies with this slick little convertible and its eye-catching Corvette Yellow paint which shines with a super gloss. Interestingly, the chopped convertible top still functions normally and the car is a blast to drive, top up or down. The huge 2.3 liter engine runs a Scat crank, 48mm IDA Weber carburetors, and an RX exhaust offers a wide power envelope which Dave has been known to give full throttle at times.

Southern California will confirm the view that in these sunny climes this is a movement to rival any current automotive trend.

Unlike the hot rod and V8 crazes which are as American as apple pie, the Cal Look is not so much an American exclusive but an

Right: The crispness of this red 1966 Beetle shows how well Bugs respond to Cal Look custom work. The owner Dennis Tures from Santa Rosa, California, built this Cal Look-er himself, shaving the trim, removing the quarter windows, adding plain European blade bumpers and a Porsche-style Turbo whaletail, and repainting the perfect body in Porsche India Red. He also re-set the suspension down about three inches and added 15in Empi 8-spoke wheels painted in bright gold. The effect is dazzling and produces an ultra clean looking Bug. It is powered with a 1600cc four, running dual port heads, Weber carburetion, and color-detailed to match the Porsche Red bodywork.

One of the great innovations of the Cal Look is its simplicity and drivability. You can mix Cal Look and daily driver together and it can turn out just bitchin'. This 1965 convertible belongs to Ken Munc, the owner of the Volks Store in Santa Rosa, California, and is driven to work on sunny summer days. This stock bodied, Mars Red, convertible has been changed only slightly to get its new look. The changes center around lowered suspension and chromed 15in steel wheels fitted with 145 front and 165 rear steel radial tires. It is powered by a 1600cc four and features a custom interior.

enjoyable world-wide trend, as VWs had been sold across the globe in vast numbers.

The movement supports two major U.S. magazines and a host of smaller publications in England, France, Germany, and Australia. This renewed interest in VWs has created an industry around the Cal Look with dozens of shops specializing in Cal Look equipment and restoration parts.

Companies like Johnny's Speed and Chrome in Buena Park and So. Cal Imports in Bellflower, California, along with MOFOCO in Milwaukee, Wisconsin, are specialty parts places which have been around for years serving the sport with parts and performance advice for VW enthusiasts everywhere.

There seems to be a thousand ways to build a Cal Bug, but if you study the images in this book you can then just sit back and imagine exactly what you might build. With the Cal Look, simplicity is the name of the game: less is better but more of the other can also be very exciting.

There are some basic rules but with every automotive trend there is a continual push for change so what occurs today might not be what happens tomorrow. To do a Cal Look successfully, the idea is to stay VW by trying to emulate what the factory might have done in some way if the Bug were still alive today.

A fascinating feature of the Cal Look is that each car appears very different and rarely do two look alike. The basic rules are smooth clean panels. Early model bodies on late model chassis are hot as are all forms of "air coolies": Bugs, Ghias, vans, wagons, or fast-backs. Mix-

Eric Birky's stunning looking Cal-Bug gave a new direction to the Cal- Look movement in the early '90s. The yellow scallops over the white body are balanced with the matching end-for-end Empi eight spoke wheels. To give the panels more texture, Eric had the hood, the engine cover, and the front fenders louvered and the running boards cleaned up with the side trim and rubber cover removed. The suspension has been dumped with a Select-a-Drop kit, lowering it two inches. Each headlight and taillight has been frenched into the fender creating a clean custom look by Arnold Birky, Eric's dad. This Cal-bug hit the cover of every VW book when it was built and today it still has a crispness to its lines and design.

When Brad Lang decided to go Cal, it became a long distance affair that crossed international borders. Based in Pitt Meadows, British Columbia, Canada, Brad took a stock-boxed 1967 Beetle he was going to build as a daily driver and got serious. He slammed the suspension with adjusted, custom rear spring plates and did a "cut and twist" to the front end with dropped spindles. He custom fitted late model Corvette air shocks and compressor so he could adjust the ride height to suit driving conditions. The body was revised with solid side windows, rear pop-outs, shaved turn signals, 1959 rear fenders, blade bumpers, and custom mixed purple paint. Powered by a stock 1500cc four, with Bugpack exhaust and 28mm Solex, it runs just fine. The Cal Looker has become a daily driver which has been run from Canada to California just for a weekend Bug Show.

ing late model bodies with early model fenders, engine covers, taillights, and hoods create interesting combinations.

Removal of the front quarter window vents is the most common first modification.

This style of two-tone Cal Look Bug has become very popular and many color combinations can be seen at the shows. Steve Jorge from Fremont, California, built this cool looking cruiser in Boo Berry with a white side panel. The combination is quite startling and very smart. Steve purchased the car for $400 and set it up with a lowered adjustable suspension, sway bars, and KYB shocks. It rolls on 15in Empi 5-spoke wheels and is powered by a mildly modified 1641cc four. It also features air conditioning, right side mirror, a Royal VDO gauges pack, and a Kenwood sound system for mega-base stereo sound.

This is easily done with simple tools and a kit from one of ten different suppliers. Next, the suspension is lowered, early single blade bumpers are fitted, and the paint is redone. Porsche or Empi wheels, a new interior with custom seats, door panels, carpets, and super sound system finish it off. A chopped top can be part of the look as well as a rag top.

62

When Brian Daniels and Gary Rowe joined forces to build a Sunday driver, it was to be all-out deal that would impress the girls, take home the trophies, and make driving as much fun as cruising. Gary started the bodywork by lopping off the top and shaving all the trim, horn vent, and door handles. The windscreen posts were molded off and the cut edges were wrapped in steel while the door edges use round tube to box the edges together smoothly. The wheel packaging was simply done with stock wheels painted Pearl Green and factory hubcaps trimmed in pink. A stock chrome beauty ring was used as a highlight. Brian was elected the paint man and he selected Bright White urethane as the base coat with Green Pearl for the slick looking scallops. The Pearl Green scallop edges were highlighted in hot pink to give the division a clearer separation and more detailed look. The body was completed with a set of Euro-Blade bumpers. A stock 1300cc Type 1 engine remains but with a lovely array of color and chrome. The interior work is all simple stuff that has been extremely well executed. The seats and the door panels were trimmed in light grey fabric over a Charcoal loop pile carpet while a neon green Grant steering wheel was modified to suit.

Terry Maheuron's wild custom VW "Rodbuster" was one of the most innovative and perfectly executed Bug projects of the past few years. Its wickedly slick looks hide an all-VW heart designed by the guys at D&D Specialties in Van Buren, Arkansas, who completed the majority of the bodywork. Denny and Dale Johns at D&D sold the project to Maheuron who finished it. Rodbuster uses a 1971 floor pan and running gear with Sway-A-Way adjusters and Jatech Forged lower spindles. The rear suspension and transaxle feature a 1971 IRS unit which was lowered one spline. The body is a 1961 convertible with the fenders, exterior chrome, and handles shaved. The hood was reformed into a solid nose section with the inner fender panels now forming body panels. A removable Carson-style black fabric top includes a 5.5in chop out of the windscreen frame and the doors are reversed into suicide-style using 1955 Chevy hinges. The engine cover is also smoothed and heavily louvered to match the new lines. Perfect Lipstick Red Delton enamel paintwork completes the bodywork. Inside are Fiero headrest speaker seats with matching center console, door trims, and carpet. Powering Rodbuster is a fairly stock 1600cc air coolie using a smoothed off 36 horsepower fan shroud, chrome valve covers, twin 34 ICT Webers, an 009 Bosch dizzy, and a matching billet fan mount and pulley.

Improved performance from the air-cooled flat four is a matter of taste rather than necessity. It is more in line to have a hip looking engine bay than to have a killer engine but if the two can be blended, all the better.

The Cal Look is one of the simplest auto customizing ideas that has ever evolved. With a huge parts industry to support it and prices that are reasonable, and as long as there's a VW to use, the Cal Look can be transplanted just about anywhere in the world.

When Philip Pinella considered building a hot rod VW roadster, his friends told him he was crazy. To prove he wasn't, he did it. Built out of a 1963 sedan, the roadster has the look of a hot rod and a Hebmüller. The pan is stock with a '67 transaxle running lowered torsion bars at both ends. The body was built from a combination BGF Hebmüller kit and stock steel pieces trimmed with custom lights and steel panels which add ribs into the rear wheel wells similar to '32 Ford roadsters. It rolls on 15in reproduction Kelsey-Hayes wire wheels. Power is delivered from a full-race, show-decorated 2180cc flat-four, with induction supplied via a pair of 40mm Delortos.

Top: Alan Papp spied a Benetton Formula One car, with its wild and daring multi-colored paint work and driven by Gerhard Berger, flying down the back straight at the 1986 Mexico Grand Prix. This wild style immediately snapped on Alan's Cal Bug thinking. Within a month he was working on his own variation using a 1968 sedan. He shaved the front fender, mounted turn signals, removed the external gas cap filler and all the factory trim along with the trunk handle. With the help of his brother he then carefully prepared the layout on the artwork as each of the eight different colors had to be separately taped and cut to get a sharp edged, ragged paintbrush look. The white base coat was then highlighted with twenty-two stripes in five different colors splashed on to the sides and roof. The splashes of color were carried over into the interior with trick multi-colored door panels highlighting the relatively stock all black interior. Alan is also responsible for the door panels which he stitched up from perforated and patterned velour, adding the dashes of color with textured vinyl. Powering the Bug is a late model fuel injection 1600 engine. It has been extensively modified with the removal of the fuel injection and converted to a 1641cc carburetored motor.

Bottom: Pat Friel is not your typical California Bug freak. He builds his cars for three reasons - show, cruising, and racing. Pat stripped his well cared for '69 sedan down to basics. The suspension was lowered three inches with adjustable coil/over gas shocks in the rear while the front was set up with '73 Karmann-Ghia spindles and disc brakes and Porsche 15in "Cookie Cutters" alloy wheels. Pat had Rick Eicher from Sonoma, California, whip out his powersaw and slice four inches from the roof in a flat chop, lop off the rain gutters, fill and weld the bumpers, french the number plate and shave off the remaining trim. The Shamrock Green Centari paint is set up with fiery silver blue, five color "ghost flames." Hiding under the removable engine cover is a 185 horse, 2180cc flat four from Engine Masters in Sonoma, California. It uses a Claudes stroker crank and ten to one compression NPR thickwall pistons. The

induction department is managed with a pair of 48mm IDA Weber carburetors mounted on a set of Scat Track tall inlet manifolds. The sedan has run 101.2mph in 13.65 seconds at Sears Point International Raceway, and that's exactly what Pat wanted from the start.

This shortened red rocket was built for fun. It has created quite a sensation at many shows but now it's a weekend drive-about for a rock and roll roady. This little Bug creates a sensation whenever it appears. The bodywork is done to a tee and its miniature looks give it a cartoon-quality that Roger Rabbit would have appreciated. It was built for Jack Williams at Birky's Body Shop in Santa Rosa, California, by slicing out the door section and shortening the pan. The door and cowl edges were then rolled and molded into the bodywork.

This Cal Look-er was done in Santa Rosa, California, by Chris Ward using a 1968 sedan. It features an unusual fiberglass flip nose which lifts up to reveal a spun aluminum fuel tank, chromed, painted, and lowered late model torsion bar suspension. Other neat tricks on Ward's Beetle include white window rubber, a frenched license plate in the engine cover, and DP wheels. It is painted in Turquoise Pearl Metallic and powered by a well detailed 1776cc motor.

Charles Cullom's lowrider Bug is a full-time cruiser. Charles is a Brother in the Midnighters Lowrider Club from Martinez, California, and is their only bug-owning member. Converting the Volkswagen's torsion bar suspension to hydraulics was an involved task. The rams are attached to the lower shock mount and are fitted into a custom-made upper suspension tower. Charles installed a hydraulic lift kit all round with a multi-direction controller for the suspension, which can be jacked up at all four corners, dropped at the front or rear, or kicked left to right. It now rolls on Star-Spoke wire wheels capped with 5.20x13 Premium Sportway tires with buff white walls. The body is reworked with a Rolls Royce-style hood and grille, Ford Pinto taillights, and Pearl Yellow Flake paint. This Bug has won many awards and is still driven most summer weekends; anywhere it goes it always draws a crowd.

Michael Doehme's 1973 Maroon Super Beetle has MacPherson strut—not a favorite among the Cal Look set but another example of how easily a good looking Bug can be built by dropping the suspension, adding Porsche 914 wheels, zipping off the chrome, and adding a new paint scheme.

This stunning engine bay is in the back of Leeroy Coleman's 1971 Super Beetle show car. It innovatively uses a Porsche 911 fan shroud assembly which Leeroy adapted to suit his VW engine. Twin, twin-choke downdrafts, a lick of chrome plating, and a mixture of blue and purple paint create a stunning engine compartment that drew raves from the crowd and a shelf full of trophies too.

The Cal Look idea is also hot in Japan with many stock and custom VWs being exported there during the past five years. The rework of a 1973 Type 3 Notchback belonging to Nobuhiro Furuya produced an interesting Cal Look-er. Built by the Day Dream Garage in Nakano, Japan, it features quad-colored paintwork, Center Line wheels, a 1700cc engine, and a full custom interior which matches the outside body colors in purples and pinks. This car was photographed at the Mooneyes Street Car Nationals in Tokyo, Japan.

Left: Richard Nischwitz's wild custom 1974 Beetle called "Zip-N" was built in Arnold, Missouri. It features a chopped top and a wild purple and green paint scheme which is split with a yellow zipper graphic. Both front and rear fenders have been replaced with fiberglass panels which are three inches wider than the originals, and a custom fiberglass running board fits between the fenders. Richard powered his Cal Look with a 1975 AS 21 "air coolie" which has been reworked to 1776cc, running dual port heads and twin IDF Weber carburetors. Richard not only cruises the shows with this Looker but he has run at the drags too, turning 16.41 seconds at 89mph.

Not all Cal Bugs are show bugs. This Hawaiian surf Bug is used every day for touring the best surf spots on Maui, rolling on Empi 8-spokes. It mixes a flat windshield body with 1974 fenders and lights.

Chapter 6

Baja and Buggies

Whereas the Cal Look goes cool and low, at the other end of the spectrum is the Baja Bug which is hot and high. The Baja Bug was developed for racing in the Baja 1000 off-road race down the Baja California Peninsula in Mexico. Racers had found that dune buggies worked fine in this race but stock bodied Bugs would get hung up running in and out of rocky crossings.

At first, to solve this problem they simply cut off the sheet metal but within a short period of time, Miller/Haven came up with a fiberglass panel conversion. This kit re-mounted the headlights into the nose of the car and opened up the wheel wells for off-road tires. The Baja Bugs became a racing class of their own and over the years many have been built for street and off-road activities.

Before all this Baja madness, came the tube-framed buggies used on the sand dunes at places like Pismo Beach, California. At first there were front-engine, four-cylinder, and V8 buggies but soon folks realised the advantages of a rear-engine, rear wheel drive. The Chevrolet Corvair flat six-engines attracted much of this attention as they offered power and a transaxle which were easy to install with plenty of tuning parts readily available.

Other buggy builders saw a different scheme of things and so evolved the VW-powered buggy. It was a lighter, easier-to-

The "Baja Bug" mutated from the "Baja 1000" dune buggy race in Mexico and instantly became a hit as a street driver back in the late sixties. Chris Gremich remembers those early days and decided to build his own street version. Using a 1958 Type 1 sedan which he'd written off in a roll-over, the project started with the bare '58 floor pan. It was then fitted with a three inch body lift and '64 Type 1 front suspension. A custom-made roll cage was fabricated and tidily molded into the new fiberglass bodywork. The Baja is finished in Orange Centari and a 2000 pound winch now sits under the flip-up nose panel. Foreign Engine Exchange in San Jose, California, built an 87 horsepower 1641cc four using a Hollenbeck counterweighted crank, CIMA forged pistons, custom heads, and a single Solex twin-throat carburetor. Power is delivered to the rear wheels via a stock '64 four speed transaxle. Chris drives the Baja to work on hot summer days and goes cruising on the weekend. Either way, he has one of the best deals going in California Baja Bugs.

Top: Some guys just want to build show cars and that's fine, but others want to build street vehicles that have just as much character and can be used to rip about off road. Mike Buegeleisen decided the only way to have the best of both was not to paint his BUGFQQT. It was therefore in a continual state of being half-finished which meant that, if he banged it up zipping around off-road, he wouldn't need weeks attempting to match the paint and missing out on the summer fun. Using a 1956 oval window he modified the floor pan so the large 38.5x15in high Ground Hawgs tires would clear the footwells leaving an open space out front where the spare tire and fuel tank used to be and lifted the body three inches for extra clearance. The suspension uses heavy duty alloy spring plates at the rear along with a 67 Bus transaxle, while the front suspension was raised three inches and KYB shocks were added. The body uses a complete fiberglass front clip which tilts and buttons up to the front cowl. The front and rear fenders, roof mounted oil cooler shroud, and visor and engine cover are also made of fiberglass. A heavy duty Bus transmission with a Super Diff running 5.14 gears helps the Baja Bug climb in and out of the rough stuff while the potent 1776cc four cylinder motor makes enough horsepower to keep it flying high with the traffic. While it might not win first prize at the state fair, it's sure to be a winner at any off road event.

Bottom: This cool looking, street driven Baja has just been finished in Vacaville, California. Ron Huff decided he would work out a plan to build a neck-snapping-head turner. Using a 1956 Beetle he spliced in a four inch body lift, converted the rear end to IRS suspension, added a Bus transmission and a raised front end. The Baja look was completed with a five piece fiberglass kit and huge BF Goodrich Super Swamper tires. Ron built up a 1600cc four, with twin Delorto 40mm carburetors and Stinger exhaust for wide-band performance. The Baja

Bug is finished in Zebra stripe paint in black and white. It is a startling combination highlighted by the chrome wheels and yellow driving light covers, mounted over the ragtop roof.

When James Gebert wanted a buggy he didn't mean horsedrawn, he meant Bug Powered. His custom-built tube framed sand buggy is street legal and driven most summers days. We photographed him in DuQuoin, Illinois, at the Street Machine Nationals after he'd driven several hundred miles from his home in Fredericktown, Missouri. The buggy is powered by a twin-carburetored, 1968 1600cc four with a Stinger exhaust. It also features an aluminum beer keg for a fuel tank, twin racing bucket seats, four-point safety harnesses, and a polished aluminum roof panel. The powertrain offers plenty of snap for on-road driving and off-road thrashing.

build vehicle that could be fabricated at home without the need to build suspension, steering, or drivetrain. The Volkswagen suspension, drivetrain, and braking was transferred into the tube frame. The evolution of sand rail racing occurred at this time which created eight- and quarter-mile tracks in the dunes for buggy racing.

Today, buggies have become sophisticated racing machines with their own classes in many forms of racing—Pikes Peak, Stadium Racing, and Baja among them.

Chapter 7

Air-Cooled Kits

The modern kit car industry owes its existence to the lowly air-cooled Volkswagen Beetle. In the fifties, when the kit car industry emerged, it was using mostly heavyweight Detroit iron, based on tube frame chassis and V8 power, with names like Woodill, Yank, Star Dust, and Rockefeller Yankee. Other innovators and designers, like Bill Devin, built kits based on Volkswagen platforms. In Australia and South Africa, kit car manufacturers were building VW based kits which filled local markets with some success.

It wasn't until 1966 that anyone successfully marketed a VW-based kit car. Bruce Meyers, a Southern California boat builder and craftsman, turned his hand to building a fun car for himself to drive on the dunes at Pismo Beach.

A rare seventies VW kit was the "Bug Box." Sold by a company in Seattle, Washington, the Bug Box sat on a regular Beetle pan and was styled as a miniature 1940 Ford sedan delivery. This version was built up on a 1970 pan and now belongs to Phil Sanderson who uses it for rural U.S. Mail delivery. It rolls on Empi Sprint Star alloy wheels and is powered by a 1776cc four.

His fine eye for design and sculpturing skills produced a fiberglass dune buggy body and within a year he'd built twelve for friends and customers using tube frames with VW suspension and powertrain. However, they cost too much to create so he began building a simpler version. In a creative move he shortened the Beetle pan and re-designed the car so it could be sold as a "build-it-yourself" kit. The result is the famous Meyers Manx Dune Buggy. Within two years he had sold over 6,000 kits.

Many have followed this same route but few have met with such success. The repli-car industry has flowered in the past few years, selling a mass of replicant vehicles using the same shortened pan concept. Porsche 356 Speedster kits have been the most successful so far and other variations include Bugatti, Frazer-Nash, Alfa Romeo, Jaguar, Mercedes, MG, and Model T Fords, using either stock or shortened pans. Original designs have also been sold including the Bradley, Fiber Jet Sand Hopper, Sterling, and Fiberfab.

The story of air-cooled VW kits is not a dead issue by any means. A wide variety of kits are currently available and recently CAD

Manufactured by B.G.W. Spectre in Delafield, Wisconsin, and built by Jim Stanfill, this Hebmüller look-a-like conversion kit is called the California Speedster. Unlike the original, the California Speedster is designed with a rumble seat option for the roadster so that it can carry four people. Jim added his own touches including the Hebmüller molded body line which matches the same shaped pressing in the hood and is not included in the Spectre kit. In keeping with his vintage ideas, Jim used pre-1966 fenders, bumpers at both ends, and early lights, then topped it off with a coat of brilliant '91 Dodge Stealth Red. The suspension was overhauled and an Adjust-A-Drop front end was installed. In keeping with the vintage style Jim used stock nine-slot VW rims capped with chrome trim rings and stock hub caps. Power is supplied by a 1974 1641cc running Mahle pistons and rings, C.B. Performance full flow oil pump, Empi 1 1/2 quart extra oil pan, and an Empi eight-pass external oil cooler.

Design in Lompoc, California, introduced a new two-seater roadster based on an uncut torsion bar pan called the Riot. This wildly styled roadster has the potential to be as successful as Bruce Meyers' classic dune buggy.

Paul Wilson's "The Mini-Woodie" was a job done from the heart. His custom woodie uses a stock 1959 pan with 1968 front suspension, modified with an Adjust-A-Drop kit. The rear was lowered with raised "Z" notches in the spring plates. The combination of style, body color, wood panels, skirts, visor, and trick fiberglass wheel covers make this woodie very slick. Nothing is out of proportion and the wagon retains all of its interior space. Paul used the 1940 Ford as a model picking up on proportions, style, and shapes. The sun visor was done just for the woodie, as were the rear fenders, wheel caps that hide the rim, and the matching skirts. The color is a custom mixed grey-green lacquer which Paul shot on. The roof is covered with a plastic sheeting material that has a '40s look, while the wooden body work was done in an exotic timber called "Padauk." The woodwork includes the '40s style ribbed roof liner, sliding side glass, and smooth wood door inner panels.

This style of VW Beetle-based kit car was popular in the seventies. Fraiser-Nash, Alfa Romeo, MG, and Bugatti Type 33 racing cars were the most popular models of the kit racers. They used a modified, but not shortened VW pan, suspension, and engine. This Bugatti kit belongs to John Ryan from Clearlake Oaks, California, and was restored by John after twenty years in storage. It features a 2116cc four and Kelsey-Hayes wire wheels. John repainted it in French Racing Blue with silver scallops, adding leather hood straps and period race car graphics.

Chuck Hale took five years to turn a stock bodied 1964 sedan into this gorgeous roadster pickup. Chuck did a perfect job creating a rounded windshield frame and a cabin area with a miniature hand fabricated step-side bed which looks just like a production unit with its ribbing and floating VW fenders. Chuck also modified the hood to give the nose a little more character by peaking the center and forming a grille-like structure in the hood. Powered by a 1600cc four, the pickup rolls on Empi eight-spokes and features a split tonneau cover which offers twin openings for both the engine compartment and the truck bed.

This Sterling VW-based kit car was one of the most successful exotic kits of its kind. Sold in England, Europe, Australia, and America, the Sterling uses an uncut VW pan and a fiberglass body with a one-piece lift up roof and doors. The driving position is laid back like a GTP race car and gives the driver a low level view of the road. This 1977 version runs a 1708cc four but any engine that can be adapted to a VW transaxle could be installed. Tracy Spencer owns this bright red version which is currently undergoing restoration.

Bruce Meyers and the Meyers Manx dune buggy is the all-time success story on VW kits. Bruce sold over 6,000 dune buggy kits back in the sixties and there was one on every street corner in Southern California for a while. These original dune buggies are quite rare now and will no doubt become choice collectors' cars. This modified Manx belongs to Ron Ratola from Pacifica, California, and features a 100 horsepower 1641cc four.

Above: As strange as it may seem, this Model T Ford hot rod is a VW kit car. It is styled like a conventional 1927 T pickup hot rod and is built with a tube frame, fixed convertible roof, and uses a complete VW transmission and engine hidden under the shortened truck bed in the rear. This perfectly built and detailed example belongs to Bob Hourigan from Fresno, California, and is finished in a deep red with a light grey fabric interior and Center Line wheels.

Left: This Neo-Classic Mercedes roadster replica was built about ten years ago for Dennis Brenner. It features a folding top, bucket seats, VDO instruments, and wire wheel insert caps on chrome steel wheels. Like other classic replicas this Fiberfab Gazelle-style kit uses an uncut pan, fiberglass body, and a full VW torsion bar suspension. Finished in cream with brown fenders, the roadster is used for summer touring and show events.

Left: This trike is probably the most primitive and original use of a VW Beetle pan and drivetrain. While no longer classified as an automobile this trike is all VW up to the front forks. It uses a VW pan with the front sheet metal removed. A wooden wine barrel forms a single seat ahead of the 36 horsepower engine.

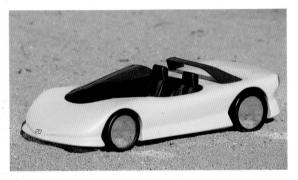

Above: From Corbett Automotive Design in Lompoc, California, Adrian Corbett's new "Riot" takes the '60s and adds the zing of a kit designed and styled in the '90s. This VW Bug-based kit can be assembled with the hand tools found in any home workshop. Its slick two-seater roadster body was designed with the able assistance of famous West Coast automotive designer Mark Stehrenberger. The Riot is designed to bolt up to any air-cooled Type I VW Beetle pan complete with suspensions, transmission, brakes, and engine and, unlike many of the VW kits from the past, the pan is not cut. The model we have pictured is a first generation 1/8th scale model which will be built in two pieces. The body will have no doors and come in one piece with a combination opening trunk lid/engine cover, and the second piece will be an interior tub.

This "Little Bugger" Beetle-based recreational vehicle was originally conceived as a project vehicle for *Popular Mechanix* magazine. A complete set of working plans were sold for a few dollars and you could build one yourself. Eventually several southern California companies began building them and sold high quality editions like this one belonging to Ken Miller from Sunriver, Oregon, for around $12,500. Ken purchased this in perfect condition and drives it regularly up and down the West Coast. He calls it his "Dirty Bugger." It features sleeping accommodation for four people, an outside shower, an icebox, a sink, a stove, and a table with seating for four.

Chapter 8

Race Cars

Air-cooled Volkswagen engines have been used to power many kinds of mechanical devices, from aircraft to motorcycles and boats. Off-road racers, use them, as well as beach buggy enthusiasts, land speed record racers, drag racers and Formula Vee.

Some are complete Volkswagens with special adaptations, others employ only the engine. Drag racing has become an all time top-line VW sport and some versions have crossed the 200 mph mark. Bonneville, with its straight line multi-mile track, is a place VWs go to play while circuit racers have runs on every kind of road course, from small rural oval tracks to huge European cir-cuits running for eight or more miles.

The Formula One circuit owes much to the lowly VW. The Formula Vee class has produced more winning Formula One drivers than any other four wheel racing class. Today in France, a new VW sedan racing class has also evolved with the help of the French VW magazine *Super VW*. It is a touring class for simply modified VWs and has grown in popularity due to its low costs.

Volkswagens and racing will continue to be part of the motorsports family as these mighty little air-cooled motors run up the revs against the clock.

Chris Bubetz races this 1964 Pro Turbo Bug built by Ron Lummus Racing using a 92in, 1010 mild steel tube chassis, featuring RLR billet aluminum motor and transmission mounts, Funny Car cage, VW torsion bar front end, and a conventional VW swing axle rear. The steel body is reworked with fiberglass rear fenders, an engine cover, and a one-piece fiberglass tilt front end. An RLR rear wing cleverly covers the expansive turbo plumbing. The interior is decked out in aluminum paneling, Beard race seat, Simpson racing harness, and Auto Meter instruments mounted both inside and on the cowl. The engine now displaces 2386cc on 1600cc Bug Pack three-piece cases using a Scat Flange crank, Pauter Machine Aluminum rods, and 94mm Venolia pistons. The induction uses a single 1150cfm Holley Dominator carburetor mounted just inside the window scoop in its own plenum chamber. The fuel/air mix is then ducted down into the Rajay HiFlow A/R.85 turbine turbo which is capable of delivering up to 26psi of boost. On the dyno it delivers 610 horsepower at 8,000 rpm. Chris has been out racing the Bug for a season and it has turned 8.93 seconds at 155.19mph in the quarter. Smaller and faster numbers are predicted for the new season but for now these numbers have the edge. That is, until the laws of physics take over.

Top: John Coffman and his wild, multi-colored Bug have had a long and glorious history of drama, performance, and hard work. The sedan was originally purchased as high school transportation, wrecked, rebuilt, and then converted to a street/race car. It features a fiberglass hood, engine cover, rear apron, fenders, front spoiler, and rear wing. John modified the rear fiberglass fenders with air pressure relieving NACA ducts and a center cut out on the rear apron for the stinger exhaust. The paint is the work of Denver Goss in Medford, Oregon. He splashed on the Candy red and solid blue base coats and then covered them with a fine set of multi-image cross-hatch and Z stripe graphics in green, blue, orange, and yellow. A new driver's side race seat was reinstalled along with a single hump roll bar and a five point safety belt. Powering up this little sedan is a hot 2180cc Type 1 engine which does not use any mechanical air cooling. The heads are from Superflow, pistons from NPR, and induction is via a pair of 48 IDA Webers. The transmission is also fully race prepped with a locker differential center. The numbers game for Coffman's 2.2 liter buzz-bomb run 190 horsepower on the dyno and these translate into 11.09 seconds at 117mph on the strip, healthy numbers in anyone's books.

Bottom: Mitch and Ray Evensen from R&R Machine in Napa, California, raced their 1954 steel bodied, glass fendered Pro Sedan for three years. It was an exceedingly fast car, turning 9.88 seconds at 135.94mph for the quarter at Bugarama in Sacramento. The Iris Mist Metallic racer featured a Pro Chassis from the Chassis Shop in Silver Lake, Michigan. It was powered by a naturally aspirated 2234cc flat-four running a Scat Prolite crank, Super Flow heads modified by R&R, two 51mm IDA Webers, and a racing Type 2 Bus transmission.

Larry Monreal's 1968 Ghia has become the fastest Ghia on the Bonneville Salt Flats and the California Dry Lakes over the past ten years. The bodywork is basically stock except for the removal of the rear center section to facilitate the quick installation of different motors and a modified trunk lid to clear the various engine heights. The Ghia's lime green bodywork and purple lettering advertise Larry's business, "Larry's Old Volks Home" in San Bernardino, California. Larry has built air and water cooled engines for his attempt records and has designed them so it is an easy change over from each type of engine. The steering is stock but the front suspension has been shimmed so it lays back. This increases the camber so the Ghia will naturally track straighter. It now rolls on special 26in high Firestones on the front and 27in Goodyear racing tires on the rear with all the wheels capped with Moon discs. Larry has collected class records virtually every year since 1977 and has managed to get 167mph out of the Ghia running a turboed 1900cc flat-four, a number which makes this the fastest stock bodied Ghia in the world.

Don Cossey hauled his 1970 Type III Fastback into Chris Alston's famous ChassisWorks after he'd managed to pare the main body shell down to an amazing ninety-eight pounds by replacing the front sheet metal with a one-piece removable fiberglass clip along with zip-on rear fenders and fiberglass doors. Chris Alston modified one of his basic Pro-1 chassis layouts to a rear engine application and then custom fabricated a chrome moly tube frame to sit under the Type III. This work included a Pro-Stock 4-link rear suspension controlled with Koni adjustable shocks and a front suspension which uses Pro-Stock Strange struts. The Type III's personal numbers now read 96in wheel base, two inches off the ground at the front and three inches at the rear. The interior is all business and most "meetings" are held for no more than ten seconds at a time. Cossey built a monster 2.8 liter "Black Rat" flat four with a custom turbo around a Bug Pak three-piece case, Scat 90mm crankshaft, Carrillo rods, and Weisco 101mm forged pistons. The induction uses a fuel injection system built by Dean Lowrey based on Hilborn components. Don has raced the Type III all over the Western United States with great success. It launches off the line like a lion pouncing on its prey. Cossey has run a 9.38 second ETs at 151mph; hot numbers for any Pro Sedan VW.

One of the Volkswagens that many VW books forget is the Formula Vee. This junior class Formula open wheel type of race car has raced around the globe for the past thirty years. Formula Vee has produced many top Formula One drivers including Emerson Fittipaldi and Niki Lauda, and Indy Car drivers A.J. Foyt and Rick Mears. This 1989 Adams Aero belonging to Douglas Agnew features "Zero Roll" suspension and a 1200cc flat-four rated at 60 horsepower. The concept of Formula Vee is that all cars are built to the same specifications and use the same stock engines. Interestingly they place the engine ahead of the stock VW transmission by reversing the ring gear in the differential. Formula Vee has the largest number of cars and the most drivers who have experienced any form of fixed class opened wheel racing.

Index

Baja Bug, 75
Boano, Mario, 47, 51
Camper, 33
Devin, Bill, 53, 79
Double-cab, 33
Exner, Virgil, 51
FiberFab, 53
Formula Vee, 91
Ghia, 29, 47
Hebmüller, 26, 47
Hirst, Ivan, 21
Hitler, Adolf, 10-13, 15
Hoffmann, Max, 26
Karmann, 26, 30, 47
Karmann-Ghia, 30, 51
Karmann-Ghia 1500, 51
KdF-Wagen, 13, 15, 17, 21
Kombi, 33

Kübelwagen (KdF Type 82), 15-17, 21, 31, 43, 44
Meyers Manx, 58 , 79
Meyers, Bruce, 53, 79, 80
Microbus, 33
Nordhoff, Heinz, 21, 26, 31, 33
Pickup, 33
Pon, Ben, 21, 26, 33
Porsche, Ferdinand, 9, 12, 13
Riot, 80
Schwimmwagen, 43, 44
The Thing, 31, 44
Transporter Type 2 Van, 21
Type 1, 31
Type 2 Transporter, 33
Type 2 Vanagon, 31
Type 3, 31
Type 60, 13